On this foundation the state is expected to erect
a fabric which shall live through the ages, a mon-
ument of the highest good, till time shall be no more.

President Alexander Martin, 1867

The grounds belonging to the institution comprise about 18 acres and form a natural park of great beauty....The scenery surrounding the site is among the most beautiful of the world. To the north and south the great Monongahela stretches away in a beautiful sheet that would delight the heart of any boatman. On the northern side of the quadrangle a little stream has carved a deep gulley, and frets over miniature cataracts to the river beyond, and around and over all tower the magnificent Alleghenies.

George M. Ford, *Monticola*, 1896

WVU's Downtown Campus

Mountaineer Statue

WEST VIRGINIA

UNIVERSITY

Photographed by Jack Mellott

HARMONY HOUSE
PUBLISHERS LOUISVILLE

Our thanks to the people of West Virginia University for all their help in the production of this book. Richard R. Polen, Executive Director of the Alumni Association, and Stephen L. Douglas, Associate Director, were especially helpful all the way through. Our thanks also to George Parkinson, Curator of the West Virginia Collection, and his staff for their help in researching the text material and printing photographs for the historical section. Special thanks to Rosemary Antol for her help in photography production.

Executive Editors: William Butler and William Strode
Director of Photography: William Strode
Hardcover International Standard Book Number: 0-916509-13-3
Library of Congress Catalog Number: 86-082735
Printed in USA by Pinaire Lithographing Corp., Louisville, Kentucky
First Edition printed 1987 by Harmony House Publishers, Louisville
P.O. Box 90, Prospect, Kentucky 40059 (502) 228-2010 / 228-4446
Copyright© 1987 by Harmony House Publishers
Photographs copyright © 1987 by Jack Mellott

PICTURES FROM AN INSTITUTION

by Dr. Ruel E. Foster
Department of English
West Virginia University

The years flow by like water and Woodburn Seminary of Morgantown, 1850 has become West Virginia University of 1987. "In my beginning is my end" observes T.S. Eliot in his poem, *Four Quartets*. West Virginia University's beginning, as most graduates know, was in the fabulous Woodburn Circle where a few male students wandered in the legendary haze of the 1860's. What the "end" of West Virginia University is to be, no one here today is prescient enough to know. Nevertheless, we do stand in Woodburn Circle today and see among the ebb and flow students from China, Japan, Korea, Norway, Sweden, France, England, Germany, Spain, Italy, Saudi Arabia, Palestine, Nigeria, Egypt and many other countries. These students bring a new cosmopolitanism to the campus. Britons use to say that if one stood long enough on the verandah of Shepheard's Hotel in Cairo, Egypt he would see everyone of importance in the world pass by. You can't quite do that on the Woodburn steps today but from those steps you can see *almost* everyone of importance in West Virginia ultimately pass by. These foreign students flow out of Chitwood, Martin and Woodburn Halls and mingle with American students from West Virginia and 47 other states. Altogether they make a grand mosaic of 18,000 students in the year 1987. They and their faculty and the Alumni are the University. The University is also a congeries of buildings—buildings lived in, worked in and played in. These well-worn structures form a not-so-frail integument of mortar and brick that fuse to form the idea of the University as a collective organism with a life of its own.

Alumni fugitives who have not seen the campus for ten years will be startled to see how completely the old Mountaineer Football Field has vanished, leaving a clear view of Sunnyside now and a great chasm where the field used to be. The friendly football crowds now travel to the Med Center to inhabit the new Mountaineer Football Field with its luxurious Press Box resting on its Easter Island concrete plinths.

If I may use one more time signal, I am the last current faculty member who walked on campus and taught here in 1941. Thus, like the "Ancient Mariner", I feel the impulse to tell from time to time the story of the University I have known so long.

The West Virginia University Campus lives two lives, as it were. There is first, its mundane everyday campus life of coming and going as we who pass through it daily see and know it. Second, there is its life as a kind of time capsule in the mind of former students who have graduated and gone out to other pursuits and been away from the buildings for years yet carry a remembered image that grows more resonant with years, like John Burgon's line on the ancient city of Petra—"a rose-red city half as old as time." The pictures in the present book are dedicated to those students who carry in their mind a lasting memory of their college days. Napoleon, quoting an old Chinese proverb, said "A picture is worth a thousand words," and, though the saying is a gray chiché at present, it expresses, as do most chichés, a lasting truth.

With the present book, one may drift back through his/her own college days and have the bitter-sweet pleasure of pushing back in time to the late 1860's when the University began and the 1870's when it was still finding its position amid the groves of Academe. If there is a presiding motif in this book, it is the motif of "place." Eudora Welty says that "Place" is "one of the lesser angels that watch over the racing hand of fiction" and what is our memory but a kind of personal fiction. "Variations on the theme of Place" might be a good alternate title of the present work. Our memories after all are bound up with the local, the specific, the significant place. All the arts are connected to place because they celebrate its mystery. The mystery lies in the fact that place has a more lasting identity than we have, and we tend to attach ourselves to identity and thus to place.

Woodburn Circle is the umbilicus from which the University has grown, and the collective memory of the University Community, past and present, cherishes this natal place by reproducing Woodburn Hall in pictures, engravings, and plates, more frequently than any other University building. It would not be too strong to say that Woodburn Hall, shown so strikingly in the following pages, has taken on for many former students the qualities of an icon, carrying with its image, strong symbolic overtones. Two stories which illustrate this come to my mind immediately. Years ago, a brisk young president, wishing to smarten up and "modernize" our downtown campus, let it be known that he planned to demolish Woodburn Hall and build something up-to-date in its place. At news of this proposal such a firestorm of indignation flared up in the state that he was compelled to reconsider and today the exterior of "Woodburn Hall" remains virtually untouched. When you think of the thousands and thousands of students who have studied in the buildings of Woodburn Circle, you realize that it is a center of immense living and immense memory. When the aged Archbishop in Willa Cather's great novel, *Death Comes for the Archbishop*, lay on his deathbed, a young cleric chided him—"You aren't going to die from a cold."

To which the Bishop replied—"No, I shall not die of a cold. I shall die of having lived." This deeply implicative phrase of the Archbishop applies with double vigor to the *mystique* of Woodburn Circle, the omphalos from which the University and so much life grew. An icon subsumes a sacred or quasi sacred character and so it was with Woodburn as my second story indicates. Some years ago, a distinguished retired professor, who had taught many years in Woodburn Hall, left instructions that his ashes be distributed from Woodburn Hall to become part of the scene he had treasured for so long a time. This was done reenforcing the veneration that clusters about these three buildings and the quadrangle. Like Walt Whitman in his poem, *Song of Myself*, the Professor could say—"If you wish to see me a hundred years hence—look under your bootsoles."

But pictures are in many ways talismanic. There is a kind of magic about them—they are swift couriers to past time. Such a book as the current one invites us to slip the cordage that ties us to the present and sail back into the old days. What was it like to drive into Morgantown in June 1941 when the air was filled with wars and the rumors of war?

I approached it by auto at twilight in late June, 1941 from the Grafton Road. The DuPont ammonia plant, needed for military explosives, was being hurriedly built with construction crews working twenty-four hours a day. One could see crews working under flood lights erecting gigantic towers. The town was full of construction workers, all extremely well paid under a cost-plus contract. The Morgan Hotel was filled as were the smaller hotels and all rooming houses. Traffic was heavy and hectic. At 10 p.m. I gave up searching and drove to Fairmont where I found a room.

Next morning, I drove in to the campus and, *mirabile dictu*, parked by Woodburn Hall (try doing that today). Woodburn Circle was quiet, almost somnolent, with a rich riot of vegetation. Occasional students in the small summer school class loitered by. It was a lazy pastoral setting of June innocence and insouciance and I would not have been surprised to see a Grecian shepherd out of the old, classic days stroll by with a shepherd's crook and a bland white lamb. I did not at that time enjoy the truncated towers of Woodburn Hall—as I now do. Inside Woodburn, I caught the odor of old wood, floor oil and the invisible presence of myriad students long since gone. On the second floor, I entered the tower office of Dr. David Dale Johnson, Chairman of the English Department. During the interview, I watched from his windows the ebb and flow of students in the circle and caught my first glance of Commencement Hall, now long since consigned to the Valhalla of used-up academic buildings. Within the hour I was employed and invited to Dr. Johnson's home on Campus Drive (behind Old Mountaineer Field) for a 3 p.m. mingling with the senior members of the English Department. At 3 p.m. I endured for an hour the scrutiny of these future colleagues, refreshed by cold lemonade—Dr. Johnson, a teetotaler, served no wine or cocktails, ever. After an hour, Professors Crocker, Bishop, Brawner, Chappell and Wentworth departed, climbing precipitous McLane Avenue to their parked cars. I noted that Morgantown hills would take a bit of getting use to and paid my devoirs to Dr. and Mrs. Johnson and left for the Bluegrass region of Kentucky.

I was back in September, 1941 to begin teaching and to see the last year of the simple, one-campus life of West Virginia University. There was no Evansdale Campus, no medical school complex, no PRT, no Coliseum, no new football stadium, no Mountainlair. Three thousand students were taught by 250 faculty members—the entire Faculty Directory had 25-30 pages. Within three months I had met virtually every faculty member. A

Personal Rapid Transit System

number of us who were unmarried, took our meals at the Faculty Club, located at that time in the Victorian house (former home of Judge Cox) at the corner of Pleasant and Spruce, now owned by attorneys Ball and Dinsmore. There were two very pleasant parlors, a comfortable dining room and kitchen on the first floor and two floors of bedrooms above. The cook was superb and there were three meals a day. It was a pleasant watering place. To lunches came Professor Harry Samuels of the Department of Physical Education. He was anxious to get into the Navy as he saw the war approaching but couldn't pass the physical. After much effort he was signed on by the Red Cross for Overseas Service and was lost in 1943 when his ship was sunk in the Indian Ocean. Cecil Highland, then a Lieutenant in the ROTC, assigned to university duty, lived there and was a pleasant companion. Dr. Fridley, of the Geology Department, lunched there and brought news of the scientific world. Professor Tony Berg, of the Agriculture School, came to breakfast to scan the newspaper for the latest news of President Roosevelt, whom he excoriated, calling down condign curses on his head on his brighter mornings. Others there, were Professor Grace Griffin, several times Acting Dean of the School of Physical Education, Professors Herbert Starr and Orval Anderson of the English Department.

During the first semester, I secured a locker in the Old Field House (now Stansbury Hall) next to a handsome, muscular young football player, named Gene Corum, later to be the varsity football coach. At times I played in pick-up games of basketball, being assigned on one occasion to guard a rotund fellow built like a Mack truck. Once he got the ball he moved like a Lamborghini sports car. His name was Scotty Hamilton, a star guard on Dyke Raese's 1942 NIT Championship team and now deceased.

But what everyone — students and faculty alike — remembers of that year is the curious undercurrent of war rumors which ran throughout the campus both semesters. Everyone was jockeying for position in the coming year. Not a week passed without a friend or acquaintance disappearing from campus to join the Air Force, Army, Navy or Marine Corps. The front hallway of Woodburn has a memorial plaque commemorating the names of those students who enlisted and died in the service of their country. Among those names is that of Roger Hicks, smallest and most fragile of basketball players, yet a first team player on the NIT championship team. The omens were there and one December twilight three of us young instructors went to a movie at the Warner Theater. We came out in full dark by the Morgan Hotel. Students were moving restlessly, incredulously up and down the street and we could hear the phrase "Pearl Harbor." We stopped at the *Dominion News* office on Pleasant Street. It was lit up and humming with excitement. All they could tell us was that Japanese planes had bombed Pearl Harbor and the results seemed bad. That was all we needed to know. A month later all enlisted. For four years West Virginia University was an adjunct of the military effort and when we returned in 1946 the pastoral innocence was gone — no one ever again fantasized of meeting a shepherd with his crook and a bland white lamb on Woodburn Circle.

But what is place without people? Without the Presidents who guided West Virginia University. In August, 1946 I returned to the campus from a four year absence in the army, to find once again the comforting world of academe plus an invitation in my mailbox to attend a great faculty dinner honoring a resolutely new President, Irvin Stewart, who was himself fresh from a prestigious war-time service in Washington in the office of Dr. Vannevar Bush (Office of Scientific Research and Development). The dinner was held in the great ballroom at the top of the Morgan Hotel. The war was over, a new and cosmopolitan President unknown to all our faculty would speak to us; a great wave of veterans were already pushing at the gates for admission in September.

All of the faculty crowded into the August hot banquet room and sweltered in the enervating humidity. Dr. Stewart, sensing everyone's discomfiture had additional fans brought in. As he rose to speak, people had difficulty hearing him over the noise of the fans. He refused their offer to turn down the fans and shouted himself hoarse but made himself heard. It was a gruelling, miserable situation for his maiden speech to the faculty. But in spite of heat, humidity and fans he made his point — a new man was aboard — the University confronted a unique and difficult situation — 6000 students were going to enroll, new teachers must be secured, money must be obtained from the state. We would not turn away a *single* qualified veteran. And we did not. We should have quailed at the announcement — no one did. Instead, led by our senior members we stood for a long ovation. We recognized a stout fellow, an omnicompetent leader — we would follow and we did. In the next twelve years Dr. Stewart fulfilled the motto of the U.S. Quartermaster Corps — "The difficult we do immediately; the impossible takes a little longer."

The Stewart era is unquestioningly the most significant period so far in the University's history. During his period, the Medical Center was launched as was the Evansdale Campus and its ancillary buildings. On the downtown campus, three new buildings were erected between the President's Home and the Old Field House. They were Armstrong, Brooks and Hodges. The faculty doubled, then tripled as did the student body. The tempo of campus life picked up. The three campuses divided the faculty — no longer was there the closeness and intimacy which had characterized faculty life of 1941-42. It was a dynamic, expansive, active period. It was a bridge from the idyllic pastoral school of the 1920's and 1930's to the more impersonal, active, crowded three-campus school of the 1960's and 70's.

Next to death, Time is man's worst enemy. Despite the expertise of cosmeticians, the preachments of nutritionists and the blandishments of Madison Avenue, Time, like the schoolboy's knife, carves his indelible initials on us all. Sir Walter Raleigh, great courtier of the first Queen Elizabeth, who had known the Queen's highest favor and then literally lost his head to King James I's executioner's axe, said it best when he wrote "For the wings of Time are tipped with the feathers of Death." But having said this, we can aver that the best alexin against Time's ravages that man has devised is photography. Old pictures show us Abraham Lincoln just as he was one July day in the New York Studio of Matthew Brady. We can see Lincoln in 1863 standing in all of his verity before a Headquarters tent with General Grant and his staff members surrounding the President. And Time bends back for each of us, and we see the same scene that the photographer saw over a hundred years ago and we feel a great élan and an impetuous joy at the miracle of time recaptured, a lost scene relived. And that is what we proffer here — "A Place to Come to — Pictures From an Institution." West Virginia University, present and past. Look on these buildings, these paths, these students and in imagination tread again the heel-gnawed steps, the myriad walks and see again the faces that once were with you in this place.

What shall we say in conclusion? We grant that Morgantown is no Petra — "no rose-red city half as old as time." Yet, if you come at sunset, in the late autumn when the campus is deserted for holiday and the deep western sun glows through the luminescent air, falling full upon the front of Woodburn Hall, as some lone student far from home loiters by, then at that moment one can imagine that Woodburn *is* a rose-red edifice half as old as Time. Language itself has been called the collective dream of mankind. And if this is so, may we not say that the university too is, in a manner of speaking, the collective dream of all the past and present generations of students — students who in their four year tenure here have left pieces and patches of their lives in some talismanic way on this campus. This book of pictures of an institution, then, is a place for them to come to in their collective dream. In some invisible way, this book, as does their campus, bears their "Kilroy was here" mark, the intimate interweaving of their school lives with their total lives. A perusal of this book can lead to their arriving where they started years ago and to know the place for the first time. And that knowing can be the beginning of something — a certain wisdom, the warm knowledge that "you can go home again," in spite of Thomas Wolfe's famous epigram. As proof, turn to the following pages.

A SELECTED CHRONOLOGY OF WVU

1862 President Abraham Lincoln signs the Morrill Act, which offers land grant of 30,000 federally owned acres for each of its congressmen to every state that agrees to establish a college providing programs in agriculture and engineering.

1867 West Virginia Legislature establishes Agricultural College of West Virginia as state's land-grant institution under the Morrill Act.. The Rev. Alexander Martin becomes the first president. Six faculty members are employed, and 184 students enroll.

1868 Name is changed to West Virginia University.

1870 First new building is completed, and is called University Hall. (In 1878 the name is changed to Preparatory Hall, and in 1889 named Martin Hall).

1873 Woodburn Female Seminary burns on site of present Woodburn Hall. The Armory is built where the mast of the battleship USS West Virginia now stands. WVU Alumni Association formed.

1876 Center section of Woodburn Hall is completed (although this building is not called Woodburn Hall until 1893).

1877 John Thompson is appointed president.

1878 The College of Law is established as the first professional school at WVU.

1882 William L. Wilson named president.

1885 Eli M. Turner named president.

1887 The forerunner of today's *Daily Athenaeum*, *The Athenaeum*, begins publishing.

1889 Enrollment of females begins. The Agricultural Experiment Station activates.

1892 Mechanical Hall and Commencement Hall are opened.

1895 James L. Goodknight appointed president. Colleges of Agriculture, Arts and Sciences and Engineering are established.

1896 The *Monticola* begins publishing.

1897 Jerome H. Raymond becomes president. The School of Music is established. The WVU preparatory school at Montgomery opens, later to be called the West Virginia Institute of Technology.

1898 First summer session is held.

1899 Mechanical Hall burns down. WVU's first farm acquired near Morgantown.

1901 Daniel B. Purinton becomes president.

1902 Library Building opens (now Stewart Hall). Two-year School of Medicine established. A second Mechanical Hall is built. A new Armory is completed on site of present parking garage behind Mountainlair.

1905 Purinton House completed.

1909 Legislature replaces individual governing boards with one board of regents to make policy for all state-supported schools.

1911 Thomas E. Hodges becomes president. U.S. President William Howard Taft speaks at the inauguration.

1912 Extension program begins.

1914 Mining extension program established. WVU enrollment exceeds 1,000 full-time students for the first time.

1916 Frank B. Trotter named president.

1918 Oglebay Hall and a basketball arena, the Ark, are completed.

1919 West Virginia Board of Education assumes control of the university. Woman's Hall (later, Stalnaker Hall) completed.

1923 Law Building (Colson Hall) completed.

1925 Chemistry Building (Clark Hall of

Chemistry) and Mountaineer Field built.

1926 School of Mines established.

1927 College of Education established.

1928 John R. Turner becomes president. Moore Hall is completed.

1929 Field House (Stansbury Hall) built.

1930 Graduate School established.

1931 New library on Downtown Campus is completed.

1935 Chauncey Boucher named president. Boreman Hall South and University High School completed.

1936 School of Pharmacy established.

1937 School of Physical Education established.

1939 Charles E. Lawall named president. Reed School of Journalism established.

1942 Mineral Industries Building, now White Hall, and Terrace Hall, now Dadisman Hall, completed. Basketball team wins national championship (NIT).

1946 Irvin Stewart becomes president. Forestry Building (Deahl Hall) acquired.

1950 Armstrong Hall completed.

1951 School of Dentistry established. Brooks Hall completed.

1952 College of Business and Economics created. Hodges Hall completed.

1957 Medical Center's Basic Sciences Building completed. Arnold Hall built.

1959 Elvis J. Starr named president. Boreman Hall North completed. Basketball team ranked number one in regular season; finishes second in NCAA.

1960 University Hospital opens. School of Nursing established. Arnold Apartments built.

1961 Engineering / Ag Sciences buildings completed.

1962 Paul Miller becomes president.

1964 Creative Arts Center established.

1965 Forestry Building (Percival Hall) and first units of Towers Residence Halls open.

1967 James G. Harlow is president. WVU celebrates 100th birthday.

1968 Creative Arts Center, Chemistry Lab, Mountainlair and Towers units completed.

1971 School of Social Work established.

1974 Law Center completed.

1977 Gene Budig becomes president. Charleston Division/WVU Medical Center completed.

1978 Energy Research center established.

1979 Personal Rapid Transit System is completed.

1980 New Mountaineer Field opens.

1981 Harry B. Heflin appointed 18th president. Shell Building opens. E. Gordon Gee named 19th president.

1984 University Hospital becomes non-profit corporation, and Mrs. Hazel Ruby McQuain pledges largest private gift in WVU history, $8 million, to its development.

1985 Barbara Schamberger becomes first woman and 20th WVU student to win a Rhodes Scholarship.

1986 Neil S. Bucklew named president. Erickson Alumni Center is completed.

Wise Library

It is a primary duty of the University to instill into all of its members — above all into the students whose responsibility it will be to continue its beneficent work — a sense of membership in and responsibility to the larger community, the community of the past and of the future, the community of learning and philosophy, art and science.

Dr. Henry Steele Commager, WVU Commencement address, June 1963

Stewart Hall

Chitwood Hall

Evansdale Campus skyline

Evansdale Library

*Upon the spot where the old Woodburn Seminary once stood,
the morning sun's rays are glinted back from the stately steeples
of such a college as may well cause the hearts of its founders
to beat proudly within their breasts.*

George M. Ford, 1896 *Monticola*

The state and the people of West Virginia have a great asset in West Virginia University. We believe your University represents the state's most prized investment and its best hope for the social and economic well-being of the citizens of West Virginia. We firmly believe that West Virginia will recognize the necessity of preserving and strengthening its great investment in its flagship University.

From "The Report of the Benedum Study Project at West Virginia University," 1984

Colson Hall

In the order of first things first, I place the faculty foremost in these plans. I place it before buildings and equipment. The greatest teacher of all time was without these, as was also the barefooted old man who walked the streets of the beautiful city on the Aegean and stopped idle talkers to inquire "What is justice?" "What is beauty?" What is truth?"

John Roscoe Turner, Inaugural address, 1929

Tomchin Planetarium, Hodges Hall

Early in the afternoon I walked out upon the campus and took position at the corner of Martin Hall in a line of students that extended to the office of the registrar at the southeast end of Woodburn Hall. While I stood in the long line, there was ample time to view great edifices that surrounded me. Oglebay Hall seemed to be the finest and most beautiful of all; her pillars standing tall, her clear, clean walls reflecting the light of day, great enough in magnitude to be the home of a deity.

Berlin Basil Chapman in *West Virginia University, A Memoir*, 1975

Stewart Hall

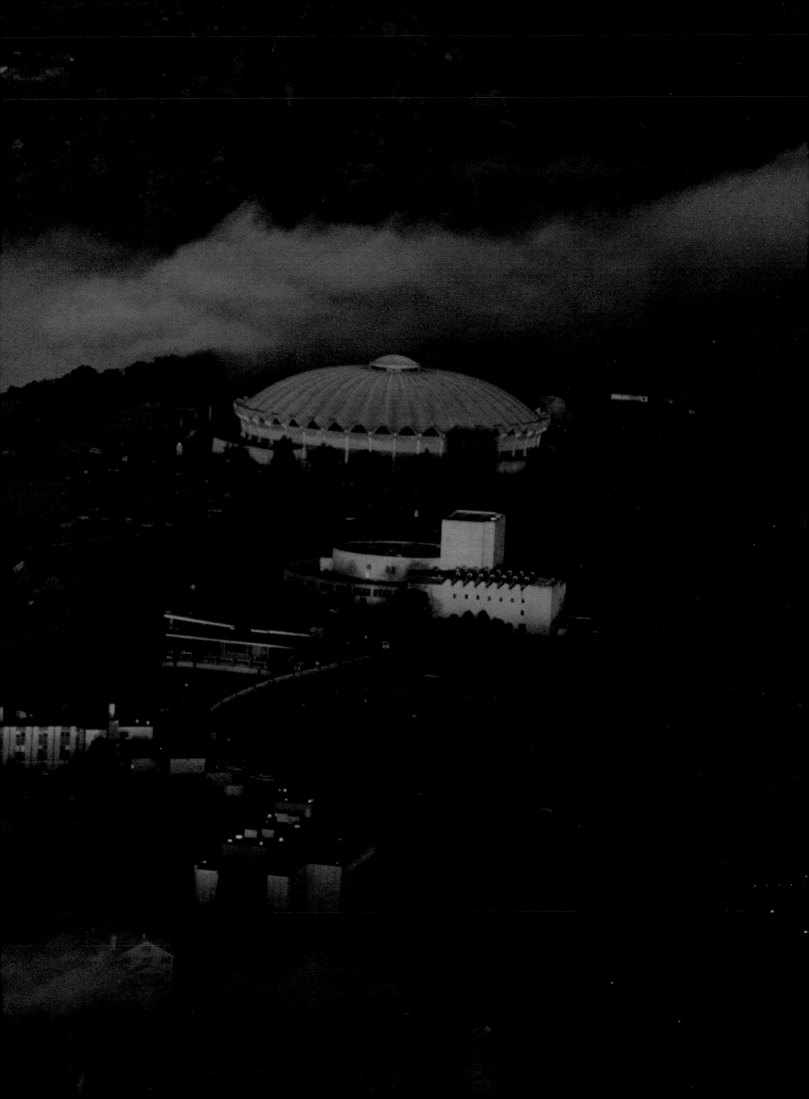

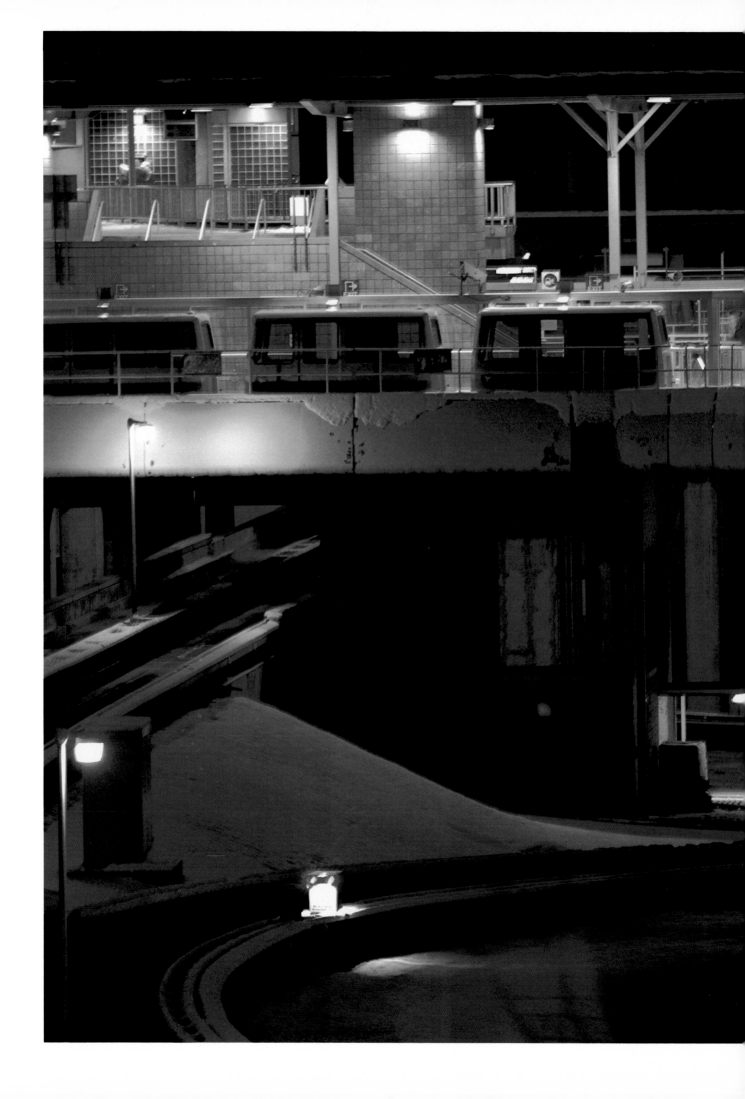

We forget those last-minute attempts to consolidate a semester's learning in a single night so that the next morning's exam could be taken in stride, yet manage to remember that favorite professor who, like us, didn't take exams too seriously. College days, ah yes, that was the life! And nowhere but nowhere could it have been lived like it was but at good ol' Alma Mater.

Peter Kalis, in *West Virginia University, A Pictorial History* , 1980

WVU Rifle Team

Cooper's Rock State Forest

In the history and ideals, therefore, which have clung about the origin and development of this university, there is reason for genuine satisfaction not only to the citizens of West Virginia but to every student of education who desires to see the orderly progress of an institution whose aims and purposes are practically identical with those of the commonwealth itself.

William O. Thompson, President, Ohio State University, November, 1911

Homecoming Parade

Tailgating, Mountaineer Field

Great though it is in intrinsic value, this stadium is greater still in its exemplification of the indomitable will and unselfish purpose that have always been characteristic of our mountain people.

Gov. Howard M. Gore, dedication of Old Mountaineer Field, 1925

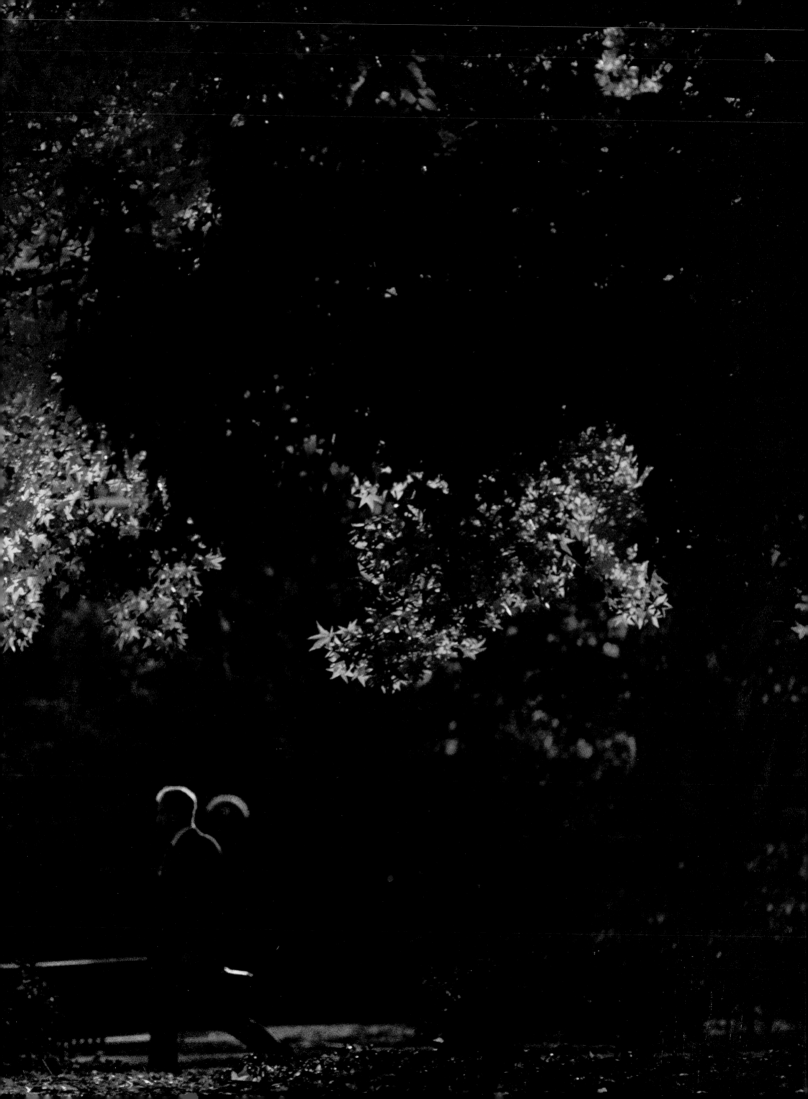

The MountainLair

At the Tomchin Planetarium

Clark Hall

71

Colson Hall

What a delightful mixture of romance and reality the scenes on the campus present . . . The campus is yet greener than was ever sung by college poet. The bordering trees are ablaze with the splender of autumn, their verdant summer foliage has been turned into myriad pennants of purple and gold. On three sides the rounded hills rise in green and fertile slopes to majestic heights. As the student stands for the first time amid this wealth of scenery, it seems to him that nature in her generous autumn mood, robed in her rich garments, has taken cognizance of his entrance to college and conspired with the University authorities to make the opening of his career auspicious.

Monticola, 1900

Martin Hall

Purinton House

There is no danger in sending our young women to the University, for the best of decency prevails in Morgantown.

Martinsburg Independent, 1889

West Virginia University's fine showing in the Rhodes competition shouldn't be considered the surprise that so many account it. A little digging turns up the fact that there is and has been a real tradition of intellectual excellence here, reaching back well into the 19th century.

Dr. Ruel E. Foster, *Alumni News*, Spring 1967

Lugar Court Room, College of Law

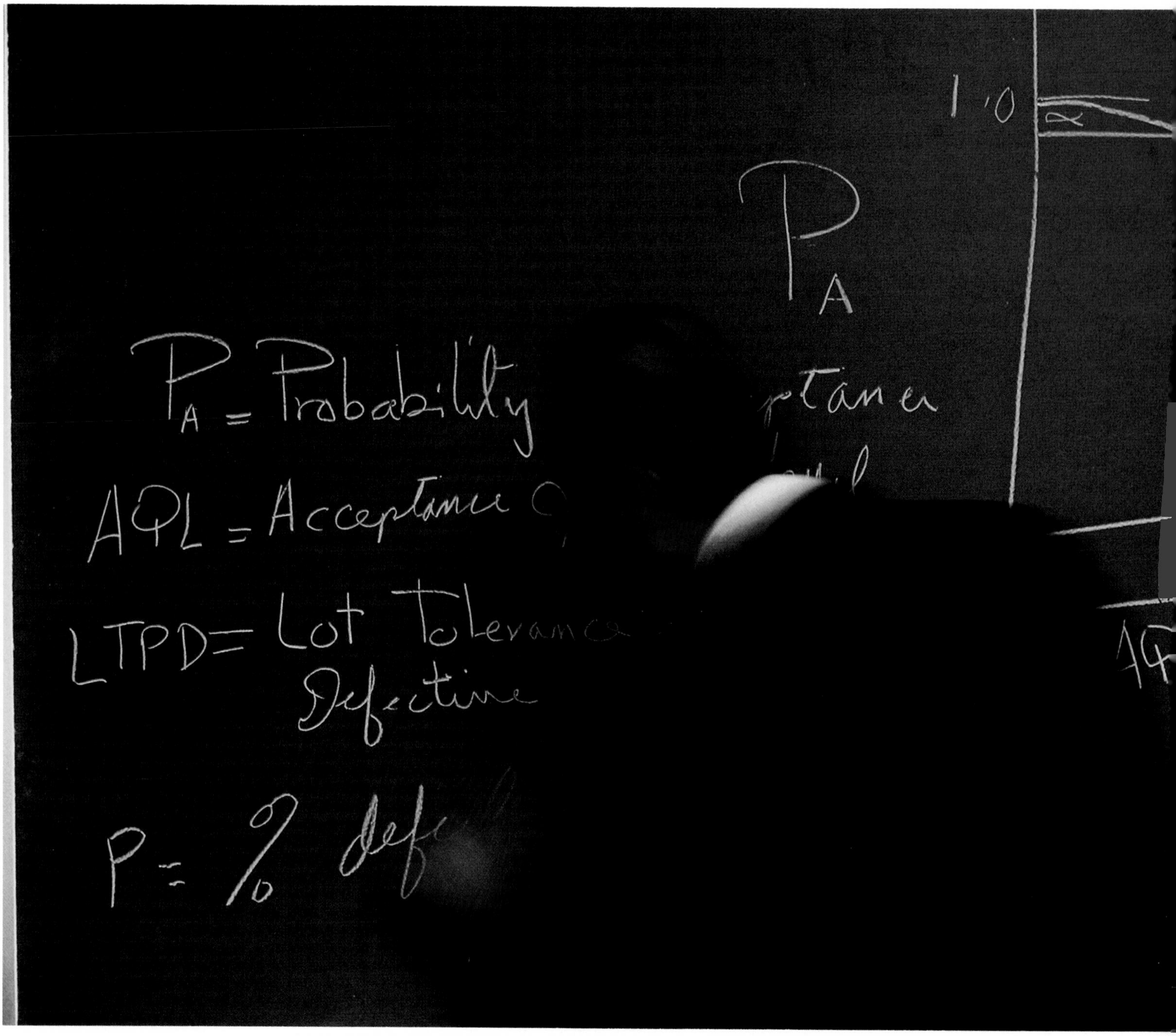
1.0
P A
P A = Probability
AQL = Acceptance
LTPD = Lot Tolerance
Defective

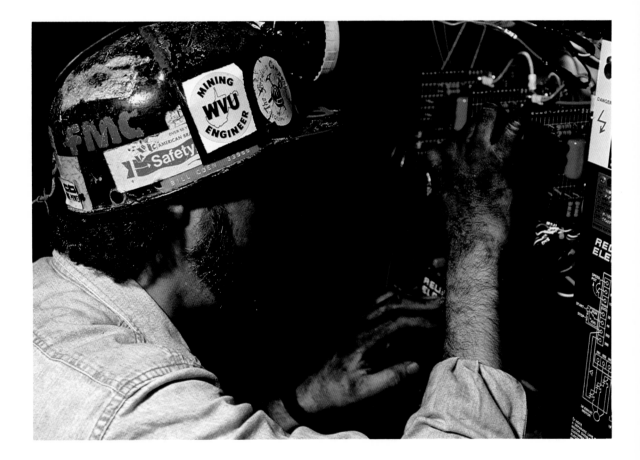

82 years ago my parents were born near Charleston, and as a child I listened to their stories and built them into a fairyland. Even now, in my mind's eye, I see this land with a sort of halo around it. Somehow, it is high up in the horizon, and I hear the far-off musical murmur of mountain streams.

Dr. Fletcher Dresslar, U.S. Bureau of Education, November 1911

Woodburn Hall

Overleaf: The Coliseum

89

It would be a brave president who would take liberties with this occasion. We have brought it all straight from the past. It is almost the most continuous link that we have with the ritual of the medieval age. With all this talk of a changing world, this is one form to which we continually cling. It is true that universities have changed vastly since the establishment of the University of Paris in the eleventh century, but we have held fast to this ancient form. This is one outward symbol that shows the close relationship between West Virginia University today and the Universities of Paris, Bologna, Oxford, Cambridge, Harvard and all the rest. We are all of a piece.

Dr. Walter A. Jessup, Commencement, 1938

You, the graduates we see before us, are the embodiment not only of West Virginia University, but also of the society at large. In you will live the intellectual and civic heritage of this institution, and in your acts and choices will flow back to the culture what West Virginia University can contribute. And in so doing, the purpose for which this University was established will not merely be a chartered wish, but a living actuality.

Dr. Gordon Gee, Commencement, 1984

LOOKING BACK

AT WEST VIRGINIA UNIVERSITY
IN PHOTOS FROM THE ARCHIVES

Photos courtesy of The West Virginia Collection, George Parkinson, Curator.

This 1872 photograph shows West Virginia University's oldest building, Martin Hall, two years after its construction. The Woodburn Seminary, which burned in the following year, stands at left.

Even should the present generation fail to appreciate, improve and increase its power, it will still live, and coming ages shall build on the foundation which here, with faith and prayer, we lay — a foundation whose majestic proportions may exceed our most sanguine expectations.

Rev. Alexander Martin, Inaugural Address, June 1867

West Virginia University's first classes were held in this building, the former Monongalia Academy, which was established in 1831. Martin Hall was built from the proceeds of the sale of this building.

This view of Martin Hall and Woodburn Seminary was taken after the fire of 1873.

The cadet corps in formation next to the Armory in 1876. The area known now as Woodburn Circle is defined by the white fence. Note also the porch and balcony on Martin Hall.

Woodburn Hall was completed in 1876, on the site of the old Woodburn Seminary. This building was first called New Hall, then University Hall, becoming Woodburn Hall in 1902.

The old Monogalia Academy building burns in 1897, despite the help of many university students.

This distinguished group was known as the Pool Forte Eating Club, and they gathered for this picture in 1893.

On the field by the Armory and the Agricultural Experiment Station, West Virginia University's first football team poses in formation for this photograph in 1891.

Workmen in 1898 begin excavation work on the north wing of Martin Hall.

At the time of this picture, Martin Hall was called Preparatory Hall. The Seth Thomas clock was put on the cupola of this building in 1884, and then was moved to Woodburn Hall in 1911.

The writing on the blackboard indicates that this is a class in Economic Science for the 1894-95 academic year.

Stewart Hall in 1902, housing the first separate library building.

Woodburn Hall, with its north wing finished in 1900.

A memorable musical event for Morgantown was the 1904 concert of internationally-famed musicians Richard Strauss, center, and Victor Herbert, right.

Morgantown has immense enthusiasm, a sincere desire toward music, and an intelligent comprehension as to the relation of music to life. It has, too...a beautiful location and a world of country about, from which to draw sympathy and audiences.

Richard Strauss, in *The Musical Courier*, 1904

In 1902, this library was built in what is now called Stewart Hall.

The fuel for a pre-game bonfire is gathered on the old Athletic Field, where the MountainLair and the Parking Garage now stand. The year was 1909, and the game was with Washington and Jefferson College, who won the contest 18-0.

President William Howard Taft attended the November 3, 1911 inauguration of WVU's eighth president, Thomas E. Hodges. The President stands, center, for a formal portrait of the attendees after a parade on High Street.

Taft also attends a reception in his honor in front of Martin Hall.

Many Mountaineer fans will remember the original Mountaineer Field, shown here in the 1920s.

Mountaineer Field under construction in the early 1920s.

Oglebay Hall looked like this in 1918. Street parking was a problem even then.

Look carefully and you'll recognize the front of the Library, shown here as it looked just after completion in 1931.

This was Reynolds Hall in the 1920s.